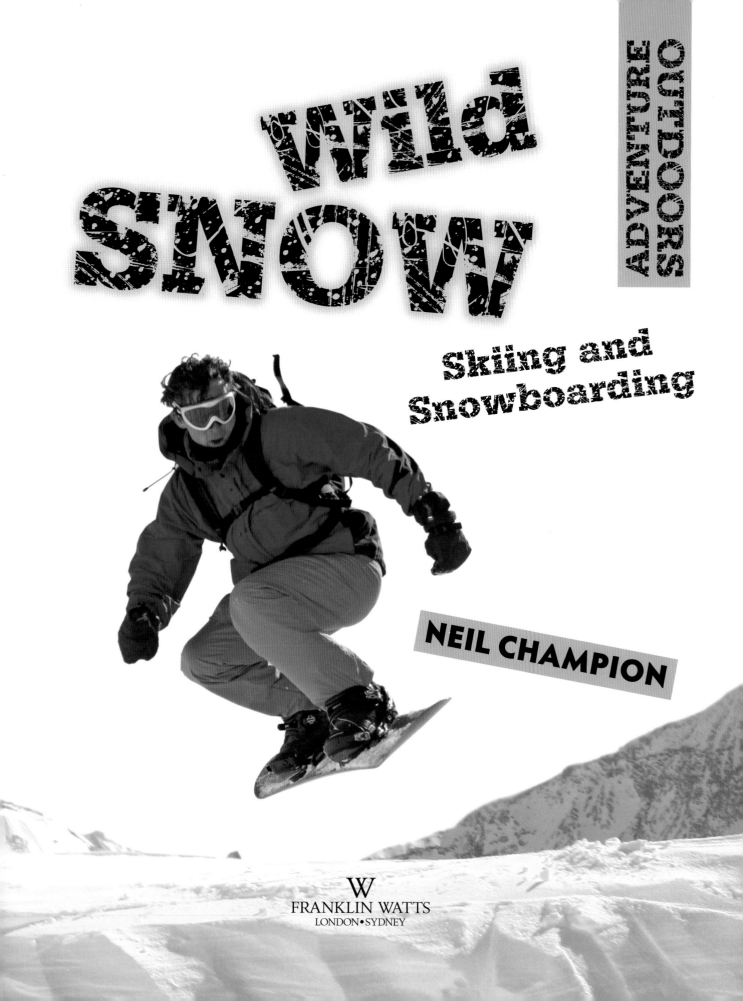

Wild SNOW

Skiing and Snowboarding

NEIL CHAMPION

W
FRANKLIN WATTS
LONDON • SYDNEY

An Appleseed Editions book

First published in 2012 by Franklin Watts
338 Euston Road, London NW1 3BH

Franklin Watts Australia
Hachette Children's Books
Level 17/207 Kent St, Sydney, NSW 2000

© 2012 Appleseed Editions

Created by Appleseed Editions Ltd,
Well House, Friars Hill, Guestling,
East Sussex TN35 4ET

Designed and illustrated by Guy Callaby
Edited by Mary-Jane Wilkins
Picture research by Su Alexander

ISBN 978 1 4451 0973 2

Dewey Classification: 796.9 '3

A CIP catalogue for this book is available
from the British Library.

Picture credits
l = left, r = right, c = centre, t = top, b = bottom

Page 1 Schalke Fotografie/Shutterstock; 2 Thinkstock; 4 Digital Vision/
Thinkstock; 5 Getty Images/Thinkstock; 6l Thinkstock, r Wikimedia
Commons/ Adrian8/Flickr; 7t Christophe Jossic/Shutterstock, bl Morgan
Lane Photography/Shutterstock, br Trekandshoot/Shutterstock;
8t Thinkstock, b Eric Isselée/Shutterstock; 9l Thomas Northcut/
Thinkstock, c & r Stockbyte/Thinkstock; 10 Gorilla/Shutterstock;
11l Demiter Petrov/Shutterstock, r Marcel Jancovic/Shutterstock;
12 Karl Weatherly/Thinkstock; 14 & 15 Thinkstock; 16t Photos.com/
Thinkstock, b Galyna Andrushko/Shutterstock; 17 Thinkstock;
18t Steve Estvanik/Shutterstock, b Maxx-Studio/Shutterstock;
19, 20 & 21 Thinkstock; 22t Tan Wei Ming/Shutterstock, c Titus
Manea/Shutterstock, b Tomtsya/Shutterstock; 23l Elena Elisseeva/
Shutterstock, r Daniel Wiedemann/Shutterstock; 24-25 Jupiterimages/
Thinkstock, 25 Thinkstock; 26 Thinkstock; 27t Tyler Olson/
Shutterstock, b Kaleb Timberlake/Shutterstock; 28t Steffen Foerster/
Shutterstock, b Thinkstock; 29 Jupiterimages/Thinkstock;
31 NotarYES/Shutterstock; 32t Andrey Armyagov/Shutterstock,
b Fedor Selivanov/Shutterstock.

Front cover: Taavi Toomasson/Shutterstock

Printed in Singapore

Franklin Watts is a division
of Hachette Children's Books,
an Hachette UK company.
www.hachette.co.uk

Contents

Let's go skiing!   4

Getting started   6

Skiing kit   8

Snowboarding kit   10

Getting fit   12

Learning to ski   14

Learning to snowboard   16

Thinking about safety   18

Hitting the slopes   20

Where to go   22

Cross-country skiing   24

Competitions   26

What do you know about snow sports?   28

Glossary   30

Websites and books   31

Index   32

Let's go skiing!

You can enjoy snow sports on every one of the seven **continents** on Earth. There are mountains and snowy places all around the world where you can ski or snowboard, experiencing the **adrenalin** rush of gliding at speed across a magical landscape.

Amazing FACTS

People have used skis, sledges and snowshoes for more than 20,000 years. Years ago, the world was much colder; snow and ice covered much more of the landscape than it does today. Cave drawings by the first early humans, known as Cro-Magnons, show them on skis. So people were moving around on skis before wheels were invented.

Roald Amundsen was a Norwegian explorer. He was born in a land of snow and ice and was a very good skier. On 14 December 1911 he and four companions became the first people to reach the **South Pole**. They had been racing a British team, lead by Captain Robert Falcon Scott. Scott's team was still nearly 500 kilometres away and although they eventually reached the South Pole, they all died of cold, hunger and exhaustion on the return journey. One reason Amundsen and his men survived was because they were much better skiers than the British men. They covered the 1,190 kilometres across **Antarctica** much faster and using far less energy than the British.

Taking up the challenge

Before you start you need to learn the skills which will keep you safe – not just skiing and snowboarding techniques, but also how to get fit, how to read a snowy landscape and how to stay warm in cold conditions. You also need some first aid skills and to know about the weather and how it can affect you in snowy places.

Getting started

Snow sports can be expensive. You need to travel to places where there is enough snow and you need the right equipment. You may also need to buy a **lift pass** to travel up the slopes so you can ski or snowboard down again.

Chairlifts carry people and their skis to the top of the slopes.

TRUE Survivors

Being disabled is no barrier to becoming a skier. Heath Calhoun was an airborne ranger in the US military in Iraq when his Humvee was hit during a rocket attack. His legs were so badly injured that they had to be amputated above the knee. Once he recovered he decided to try skiing. Four years later he had become good enough at ski racing to take part in the 2010 Winter **Paralympics**.

Heath Calhoun carries the US flag at the Winter Paralympics.

An artificial ski slope is a great place to practise snow sports.

Ski clubs

Ski clubs offer information on the best **ski resorts** and the condition of the snow there. Snowfall varies from one year to the next. Ski clubs will also put you in touch with people who love the sport and can help you get started. You may be able to find cheap equipment and have some lessons through them.

Artificial ski slopes

A great way to spend time on the slopes without travelling hundreds of kilometres to the mountains is to use an artificial (or dry) ski slope. The earliest artificial slopes were made from bristly tiles and plastic brushes. Skis glided over them and could dig in when you wanted to turn. The materials used today look more like snow and give a better idea of what it is like to ski on snow.

Amazing FACTS

When Europeans arrived in North America more than 400 years ago, they found that the native people in the country now called Canada used snowshoes to travel around in deep snow. In the 1500s, the French priest and explorer André Thévet described them as '...a kind of racquet, strung with cords made of the **sinews** of animals, in the form of a grid... two and a half feet long and one foot wide...'

Old-style snowshoes

Modern snowshoes

Skiing kit

The right kit is essential if you are to get the most out of your time on the slopes and you will need some expert advice on what to buy.

Clothing

Ski clothing should keep you warm when you are sitting on a ski lift or stuck in a **blizzard**. It also needs to allow your skin to breathe, because you will get warm as you use your muscles gliding downhill or pushing across a flat landscape. You need a thin warm layer against your skin: thermal vests and long johns with a fleece shirt or thin jumper over the top. On top you need a fleece jacket and windproof cagoule or a padded jacket. You also need to keep your legs warm: the temperature high in the mountains is below zero.

hat

gloves

goggles

ski suit

ski poles

skis

ski boots

Amazing FACTS

The soft down feathers next to the skin of birds are brilliant **insulators**. The feathers have a loose but strong structure which traps layers of air. Air holds heat well and keeps the birds very warm. The best down comes from geese and ducks and is used to make warm clothing and duvets.

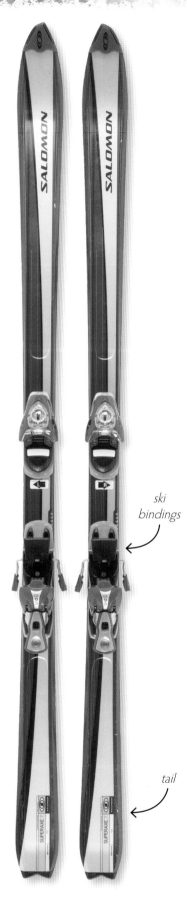

ski
bindings

tail

TRUE Survivors

In February 2011, two men were skiing in Helen Lakes in Canada. They were about 2,400m high and the temperature was well below zero. One of the men caught his ski and twisted his ankle so badly that he could not stand on it. His friend skied off to find help, but it was more than three hours before a helicopter came to pick up the injured skier. He could not move during his wait, but he did have very good clothing, including a down jacket, and plenty of food and liquid. This meant that he did not get **hypothermia**, although he needed an operation to repair his ankle.

Choosing skis and boots

Skis have a turned-up front so they don't catch in the snow and a smooth, flat base so they slide easily. The edges are sharp and metallic to bite into the snow when you turn. The longer your skis, the faster you will go. To start with, do not wear skis taller than you are. Your ski boots must fit well: you need high, rigid boots for downhill skiing (to help when turning) and smaller, lighter boots for **cross-country skiing**.

Cross-country ski boots

Downhill ski boots

Snowboarding kit

There are three main types of snowboard and you need to understand the differences between them before choosing one. Snowboarders need similar clothing to skiers.

Freestyle

Types of board

A freestyle board is great for beginners. It is wide, stable, light and short, as well as flexible. This means you can move it around and turn easily and use it for doing tricks.

Freeride boards are the most popular. They are good all-round performers, for both beginners and more experienced riders and can be used on both hard and icy or deep and powdery snow.

Freeride

Alpine

Goggles are especially useful when it is snowing.

The third type of board is an alpine. It is long, narrow and stiff, and so fast and good for carving out clean turns on wide slopes. Experienced boarders use this type of board.

Clothing

Like skiers, snowboarders wear a base layer, a mid layer and an outer layer. The mid layer can be put on or taken off depending on temperature. The outer layer protects you from the wind and snow. Don't forget gloves and a hat (most boarders wear beanies). You will also need goggles and possibly a helmet. Boarders fall more than skiers, so parts of their clothing (knees, bottom and backs) are reinforced for protection.

goggles

beanie hat

gloves

waterproof jacket

snowboarding trousers

Amazing FACTS

Snowboarding began in the USA during the 1950s, although it only became popular more than 30 years later. Keen surfers took their skills to the snow slopes on custom-made boards. The first commercial boards were sold in the 1960s. An air of rebellion was linked to the sport and boarders were not allowed on ordinary ski slopes at first. Even in 1988, very few slopes allowed boarders. Ten years later the scene changed and today most ski resorts welcome the youthful sport of snowboarding.

Young people enjoy the challenge of boarding tricks and stunts.

Getting fit

Skiing and snowboarding are much more enjoyable if you are fit before you try them. There are plenty of exercises you can do at home and in open spaces near you to improve your fitness.

Working on strength

Skiers need strong thigh (or quadriceps) muscles. These work hard as you glide downhill with your knees bent and they also power you on the flat. Squat exercises help to strengthen these muscles.

Stand upright with your legs shoulder-width apart. Put your arms out in front of you. Bend your knees until your thighs are parallel with the ground. Keep your back as straight as you can. Hold. Then stand up. Repeat this ten times, then rest for one minute, then repeat again.

Two leg Squat

A harder version of this is the one leg squat. Balance on one leg with the other held out in front. Take your arms out in front of you and bend your knee. See how low you can go and then come up without falling over. Don't try to do too many at first; build up over time.

One leg squat

To do a split squat, you stand up and lunge one leg forward, keeping your thigh parallel with the ground. Lower your back knee as close to the ground as possible. Stay there for five seconds then come up. Repeat ten times if you can.

Split squat lunge

Stretches

Stretching after exercise helps your body recover and prevents your muscles from being stiff the next day. There are several useful stretches for skiers, including the standing thigh stretch, the standing hamstring stretch, the groin stretch and the hip stretch.

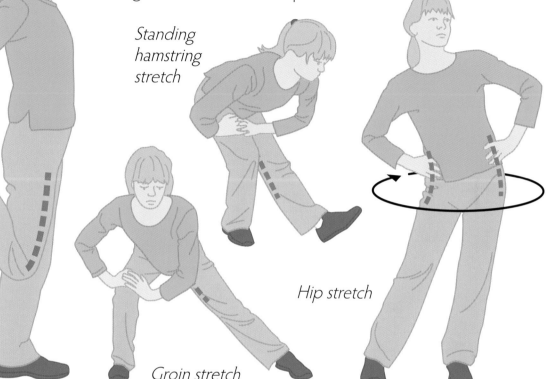

Standing thigh stretch

Standing hamstring stretch

Groin stretch

Hip stretch

Amazing FACTS

Your body responds to exercise by sending signals to the muscles you are using. Extra blood carrying energy-giving nutrients travels to the parts of the body that most need it. Other parts of the body are partly shut down. So when you exercise, less blood goes to your stomach and more goes to the muscles you are using. Your heart beats faster and your breathing rate increases so blood and oxygen move faster around your body. Eventually the muscles you are using will increase in size as they do more work and become more efficient.

Learning to ski

Making your first slide downhill on a pair of skis can be scary. You need help from experienced people and one of the easiest ways to find this is to sign up at a ski school.

Learning to balance on one ski is harder than it looks.

Basic technique

Once you put on skis, your feet will seem ten times their normal size – and they don't grip the ground, but slide over it! You need to get used to skis on flat ground. Practise turning in a circle where you stand by moving the skis. Shift your weight from one foot to the other. Try lifting one ski in the air and balancing on the other, staying loose and relaxed. This is harder than you might think. Falling over a few times will help.

Amazing FACTS

Italian Simone Origone is the fastest man on skis. He travelled at 251.4 km/h to set a world speed record in the French resort of Les Arcs in April 2006. Just one day later, at the same ski resort, Sanna Tidstrand from Norway set a new world record for the fastest woman on skis. She shot down the slopes at a maximum speed of 242.59 k/mh.

The snowplough helps you turn and slow down.

Learn to turn

You can graduate on to a gentle slope to learn how to slow down and turn using the snowplough. Try to do this without using **ski poles**. Keep your skis parallel and aim down a gentle slope. As you gather speed, push out with your heels so the tail ends of your skis move out and the tips move together. The pressure you apply to your skis will make you slow down. If you press more on one side than the other you start to turn.

TRUE Survivors

On 23 April 2007, American Barbara Hillary stood in one of the most hostile places on Earth – the North Pole. She had skied there, braving **frostbite**, hunger and polar bears. Many had done this in the past 100 years, but this woman was unique in several ways: she was 75 years old (one of the oldest to get there), she was the first black woman to reach the Pole, she had survived cancer and she had not skied before this adventure. As she said, skiing 'was not a popular sport in Harlem', where she grew up.

ARCTIC OCEAN

NORTH + POLE

80°

GREENLAND

Norw
S

son

ICELA

Learning to snowboards

Snowboarding appeals to young people partly because boarders fall over much more than skiers do. You can also do more stunts and tricks on a snowboard once you have mastered the basics.

Snowboarders stand sideways to the slope when on their boards.

Body position

Run forward in the snow and slide on your feet. The leading foot is the one you want in front on your snowboard. Buckle this one in first. On the board, distribute your weight evenly between your feet, with body and shoulders parallel to the board, and head looking forwards over your shoulder. To turn, shift your weight forward and lean on your toes or your heels, depending on which way you want to go.

Always strap your leading foot to the snowboard first.

Expect to fall over a lot when you are learning to snowboard.

Learning to fall

Plenty of skiers and snowboarders are injured every year when they fall badly. The most common injuries are to knees, ankles and wrists. Always try to fall to your toe-side, landing knees first in the snow, following with your hands clenched into a fist. This will help protect your wrists. Try to ride your board in a relaxed and flexible position, with knees bent and hands out.

TRUE Survivors

In March 2011, 24-year-old Nathan Scott was snowboarding in the Jasper National Park in the Canadian Rockies. He set off for one last big run before returning to the valley, but became lost in a vast area of snow and rock. Without food, water, map or compass, he needed help. After friends reported him missing, a rescue helicopter took nearly 24 hours to find him and return him unharmed to warmth and safety.

Thinking about safety

Sliding downhill at speed on a snowy slope is risky. When you are skiing, you need to match your level of skill with the challenge you take on.

Learning to ski at ski school with an instructor is a great way to get started.

First things first

Start by going to ski school to learn how to turn and stop on a **nursery slope**. Each level of difficulty requires greater skill and more experience. Make sure you don't take on too much before you are ready.

TRUE Survivors

In March 2011, two British skiers became lost in bad weather nearly 2,000 metres above an Italian ski resort. Charlotte Taylor and Matthew Kitchener strayed from the piste into a dangerous **ravine**.

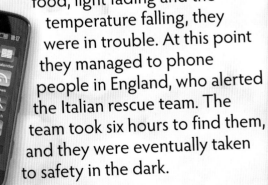

They could not see in the blizzard and were **disorientated**. With no food, light fading and the temperature falling, they were in trouble. At this point they managed to phone people in England, who alerted the Italian rescue team. The team took six hours to find them, and they were eventually taken to safety in the dark.

Hazards on the slopes

Here are the main **hazards** to watch out for.

1 Other people
Collisions can be disastrous, so keep an eye on the other people around you.

2 Losing control
This can happen quite easily, especially when you are learning how to turn.

3 Dangerous areas
Avoid trees, fences and cliffs. Some trees and fences have padding around them and cliffs may have barriers to stop you skiing over them.

5 Avalanches and white-outs
In an avalanche snow slides quickly down a slope and can carry you away and bury you. On piste slopes in ski resorts, avalanches are not usually a danger, but if you go **off-piste**, you may get caught in one. A white-out happens when it is snowing and you are in dense cloud. Everything looks white, there is no **horizon** and your senses become confused; then it is easy to become lost.

4 Losing a ski
This may happen if you catch an edge or because your skis have not been tightened so they stay connected to your boots. Overtight connections are also a problem as they may prevent your skis coming off when you fall. This can lead to a twisted knee, a common skiing injury.

Hitting the slopes

Getting on to the slopes is what skiing and snowboarding are all about. Being on a snow-covered mountain and feeling the adrenalin rush of gliding downhill is an amazing sensation.

Weather and the environment

Check the weather forecast for the day. Cloudy conditions can make it difficult to find your way, sunshine can overheat you and wind can blow snow into your eyes, so wear goggles to protect them. Don't be surprised if you feel out of breath – your body will take time to adapt to the **altitude**. Many skiers take a small rucksack with a little food and water as well as spare clothing and gloves.

TRUE Survivors

The highest point on earth is the summit of Mount Everest; 8,850m high and with not enough oxygen to sustain life. In October 2000 Slovenian Davo Karnicar skied from the summit to base camp, a distance of four kilometres and a vertical drop of around 3,500m. He took more than four hours to ski the distance in one go.

A piste-basher prepares the snow for skiers and snowboarders.

The slopes

In ski resorts machines with tracks called snowcats drive over the slopes to even out the snow. There are rope barriers near dangerous areas and trees and fences often have padding around them. You will need a map of the area showing the ski runs, as well as a lift pass.

Off-piste skiing

Skiing off-piste means travelling over wild terrain. Off-piste trails are not prepared or evened so the snow lies as it has fallen. The big risks of skiing off piste are becoming lost and being caught in an avalanche.

Ski run grades

Green Easy nursery slopes; very broad and gently sloping.

Blue Suitable for beginners, but steeper than green runs. May be longer than green runs and go through more interesting areas.

Red Suitable for intermediate skiers who can turn and stop easily. Parts of red runs may be narrow or steep.

Black The hardest runs at a resort, for expert skiers only. Very steep in places.

Where to go

Zermatt, Switzerland

There are many ideal places for snow sports around the world. Europe and North America have the most resorts, but there are resorts in Australia and New Zealand with good snow, as well as in countries such as Bolivia in South America.

Lake Wanaka, New Zealand

Europe

There are ski resorts in Norway, Slovenia, Bulgaria, Andorra and Scotland, but the most famous resorts are in France (Chamonix, Avoriaz, Val d'Isere), Switzerland (Zermatt, St Moritz), Italy (Cervinia, Cortina) and Austria (Kitzbuhel, St Anton). The slopes can be crowded in February and March, which are the peak ski and snowboarding months.

St Anton, Austria

North America

The resort of Snowbird-Alta in Utah has about 12 metres of snow a year. Breckenridge in Colorado has easy wide pistes which are great for beginners, and Jackson Hole in Wyoming has difficult runs for experts. Banff in Canada has a reputation as a good value resort for both skiing and snowboarding.

Banff, Canada

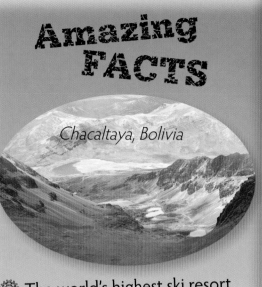

Chacaltaya, Bolivia

Amazing FACTS

❄ The world's highest ski resort is Chacaltaya in Bolivia, which is 5,421m high.

❄ The world's longest ski run is probably the Vallee Blanche near Chamonix in France. It is 22 km long and drops almost 3,000m.

❄ One of the hardest ski runs in the world is La Chavanette, or The Swiss Wall, in Avoriaz in France. It is only 1 km long, but drops 331m. A sign at the top warns: 'For experts only'.

Australia and New Zealand

The resort of Thredbo in Australia includes the country's highest peak, Mount Kosciusko (2,228m). Mount Baw Baw is another resort three hours' drive from Melbourne and a good place for beginners. The island of Tasmania has a ski resort called Ben Lomond.

New Zealand has mountains as high as 3,700m in South Island and even a volcano that you can ski or snowboard down on North Island. The Lake Wanaka region has the largest area suitable for skiing. The season here runs from June to October.

Cross-country skiing

Thousands of years ago, people used skis to travel over flat or gently sloping snow-covered ground, rather than down steep mountains. Today cross-country skiing is a popular sport for which skiers wear special footwear and skis.

TRUE Survivors

In January 2010, three cross-country skiers, Jesse, Christine and Josiah, set off to cover part of a 15 km circuit of Mallard Creek in Yellowstone National Park. A series of incidents led to near disaster. They did not take the right equipment or enough emergency gear. Once on the trail, Josiah had problems with his skis and bindings. The snow was deep (over a metre) and their skis were too small to stay on the surface. Eventually, they took off their skis and walked, getting very cold feet. Exhaustion followed and the three became separated as darkness overtook them. Fortunately, a rescue was organized when they failed to return before dark. Josiah had badly blistered and frost-nipped feet, but all made a full recovery.

Away from the crowds

If you want to get away from it all, cross-country skiing is the sport for you. You can avoid crowded high mountain resorts and ski into the wilderness. You'll need a map and compass, as well as a rucksack with emergency gear. Norway has more than 400 huts where cross-country skiers can stay, so you can explore large stretches of country on skis.

Different equipment

Only the toe of your boot is clipped to a cross-country ski. This means you can lift your heel, push off with your legs and glide across flat country using your poles. The easiest way to start is on prepared tracks or pistes where parallel lines run through the snow. You place one ski in each and go. Grooves like fish scales cut into the bottom of the ski help you move along. When you push backwards, they grip the snow. Some skis have special waxes to help them grip and you can also attach an extra layer called a **skin** to help you go uphill.

This cross-country skier has the freedom of the snowy hills to enjoy.

25

Competitions

Skiers can compete in Alpine ski events, **Nordic** or cross-country skiing and ski jumping. The Winter Olympic Games is held every four years. The International Ski Federation oversees international snow sport competitions.

Alpine events

These events include very exciting downhill racing, as well as slalom, giant slalom and super giant slalom (or Super-G). Skiers race downhill over a specially prepared course, one at a time. The fastest skier wins. The rules are simple, but the races are dangerous and crashes can be spectacular.

Slalom skiers weave between poles called gates set up on a course. If they pass a gate on the wrong side, they are knocked out. The fastest competitor who keeps to the course over two events is the winner.

Slalom

Ski jumping

Ski jumpers slide down a huge high ramp on very large skis, taking off at the end of it. The aim is to glide as far as possible, making the longest jump you can. Skiers are given points for distance, but also for the quality of their glide and landing. The world record is held by Norwegian Johan Remen Evensen; in 2011 he jumped an incredible 246.5m.

Ski jump

Snowboarding events

The International Snowboard Association sets the rules for all snowboarding competitions. The main snowboarding events in the Winter Olympics are:

Half-pipe

❋ **Half-pipe: held in a U-shaped arena, where judges award points for jumps and stunts.**

❋ **Parallel giant slalom: boarders ride down a prepared course and the boarder with the best time over two attempts wins.**

❋ **Boardercross: four to six competitors ride together down a course full of bumps and banks of snow. The first past the post wins.**

All three events have separate men's and women's competitions.

WINTER PARALYMPICS

There are snow sport competitions for disabled competitors all round the world today. The biggest event is the Winter Paralympic Games, held every four years, which began in 1976 in Sweden. Events include Alpine downhill races, slalom races and cross-country skiing.

27

What do you know about snow sports?

Are you ready to take on the challenge of skiing or snowboarding down the slopes of a mountain resort or sliding cross-country into the wilderness? Do you know the difference between a blue run and a black run? Can you remember which is the highest ski resort in the world? Try this quiz to find out how much you know about the great snowy outdoors. Answers are on page 31.

1 Which of these statements is correct?

a A beginner's skis should be taller than they are..

b You should wear goggles or sunglasses to protect your eyes.

c The edges of your skis should be sharp so you can cut into the snow to turn.

d You should have rigid legs and stiff knees when snowboarding.

e You don't need to worry about avalanches when skiing off-piste.

2 The highest ski resort in the world is in which country?

a The USA   **b** England   **c** France   **d** Bolivia

3 Snowboarding began in the USA in the 1950s
True or false?

DANGER D'AVALANCHES

DANGER OF AVALANCHES

LAWINEGEFAHR

4 A snowplough is:

a Turning the tips of your skis inwards and pushing out with your heels to slow down and make a gentle turn.

b Another name for a snowboard.

c A type of bird that lives high on snowy mountains and ploughs through the snow with its beak looking for food.

d A place where you can stop to get food and refreshments.

5 Which ski slopes are suitable for a beginner?

a Black runs   **b** Green runs   **c** Blue runs   **d** Red runs

6 A half-pipe is a snowboarding term that describes:
a A broken pipe.
b A large U-shaped arena where snowboarders do tricks and stunts.
c A place where you can relax and hang out with other snowboarders.
d A type of chairlift specially for snowboarders.

7 What does altitude mean?
a The height of something (a mountain summit, a ski resort) above sea level.
b Somebody's manner and way of speaking to other people.
c Getting really cold in the high mountain air.
d A term used by one snowboarder for another.

8 People have been skiing for more than 20,000 years
True or false?

9 Cross-country skis are much thinner than Alpine or downhill skis
True or false?

10 Name the stretch

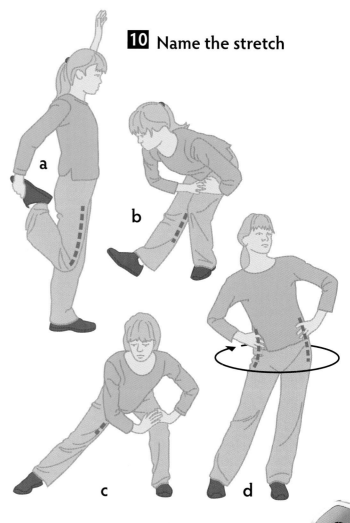

Glossary

adrenalin A chemical made in our bodies to help us run fast from danger or fight it.

altitude The height of something above sea level.

Antarctica The most southerly continent on Earth. At its centre is the South Pole.

blizzard A combination of strong wind and snow. It is very difficult to see in a blizzard.

continent One of the seven huge land masses on Earth – Asia, Africa, North America, South America, Antarctica, Europe and Australia and New Zealand.

cross-country skiing A style of skiing which is adapted to travelling across flat landscapes with gentle hills, rather than down mountains.

disorientated Being lost and not knowing which way to go.

frostbite Damage to fingers and toes caused by extreme cold.

hazard Something that can harm us. On a ski slope, hazards might include trees, fences or rocks skiers could collide with, or avalanches.

horizon The line in the distance where the sky meets the ground.

hypothermia A very dangerous condition in which someone becomes so cold that they lose consciousness and may die.

insulator Warm, windproof clothing that keeps out the cold.

lift pass A ticket you buy to travel up a mountain on ski lifts and ski chairs.

Nordic A style of skiing that grew up in Norway rather than the Alps. Cross-country skiing is a type of Nordic skiing.

nursery slopes Very gentle slopes used by ski instructors to teach complete beginners the basic skills of skiing or snowboarding.

off-piste To travel off marked ski trails and into the back country. You need to be very experienced to cope with off-piste skiing.

paralympics The Olympic games for people with disabilities.

ravine A large goudge in the side of a mountain, carved out by a river.

sinew Another word for tendons, the tough fibre in our bodies that attaches muscle to bone.

ski poles Most skiers hold a ski pole in each hand to ski down slopes.

ski resorts Specially built villages in the mountains with hotels, restaurants, ski lifts and pistes for skiers.

skins Strips of material that stick to the bottom of a ski which allow it to slide forward, but also grip the snow when pushed backwards. Cross-country skiers use skins to ski uphill.

South Pole The most southerly point on Earth, at the centre of Antarctica.

Websites

www.fis-ski.com The International Ski Federation
www.skiclub.co.uk The Great Britain Ski Club
www.ussa.org The US Ski and Snowboard Association
www.disabledskiing.ca A Canadian website for disabled skiers
www.snow.co.nz The New Zealand Snowsports Council

Books

Skiing and Snowboarding: 52 Brilliant Ideas for Fun on the Slopes
  Cathy Struthers, The Infinite Ideas Company, 2006
Total Skiing Chris Fellows, Human Kinetics, 2011
Skiing Fred Foxon, The Crowood Press Ltd, 2003

Quiz answers

1 *b and c*

2 *d*

3 *True*

4 *a*

5 *b and c*

6 *b*

7 *a*

8 *True*

9 *True*

10
a Standing thigh stretch
b Standing hamstring stretch
c Groin stretch
d Hip stretch

Index

Alpine skiing 26, 27
altitude 20, 29, 30

Amundsen, Roald
  5
Antarctica
  5, 30
artificial ski
  slopes 7
avalanches
  19, 21

boots 8, 9, 19, 25

chairlifts 6
clothing 8, 9, 10, 11, 20
competitions 26-27
cross-country skiing
  9, 24–25, 26, 27, 30

downhill skiing 9, 26, 27
dry ski slopes 7

equipment 6, 7, 24, 25
Evensen, Johan Remen 27
Everest, Mount 21
exercises 12, 13

falls 11, 14, 16, 17, 19
first aid 5
fitness 5, 12–13

goggles 8, 10, 11, 20, 28

hazards 19, 30
hypothermia 9, 30
injuries 6, 9, 17, 19

lessons 7

muscles 8, 12, 13

Nordic skiing 26
North Pole 15

off-piste skiing 19,
  21, 30
Origone, Simone 14

paralympics 6, 27, 30
Powell, Darren 16

safety 5, 18–19
Scott, Robert Falcon 5
ski clubs 7
ski jumping 26, 27
ski racing 6, 26
ski resorts 7, 11, 14, 18,
  19, 21, 22-23, 28, 31
ski run grades 21, 29
ski schools 14, 15, 18
skiing kit 8-9
skiing techniques 4,
  14, 15
skins 25, 31
skis 4, 6, 7, 8, 9, 14, 15,
  19, 24, 25, 27

slalom 26, 27
sledges 4
snowboarding events 27
snowboarding kit 10-11
snowboarding
  techniques 5, 16, 17
snowboards 10, 11
snowcats 21
snowshoes 4, 7
South Pole 5, 31
speed records 14, 16
stretches 13, 29
stunts 11, 16, 27

Tidstrand, Sanna 14

weather 5, 18, 20
white-outs 19